Quilts by
MONDAY

Edited by Carolyn S. Vagts

Annie's™

Introduction

Sometimes, it's nice to have a project that can be done in a weekend for one reason or another—one that can be pieced, quilted, bound and ready to use by Monday. Maybe you've decided to make a special gift for someone at the last minute, or maybe you just want to complete a project and bask in the glory that it *is* done.

Within these pages, you will find 12 projects that, if you put your mind to it, can be done by Monday. We have included many sizes and many skill levels. We have even included size options for those of you who are looking for a specific bed size. There's one project that could be rated "over achiever" by most, but it could be done in a weekend if you really put your mind to it. Many were created with precuts, some with scraps, but all have style and appeal. Our designers have done it again. We set the challenge, and they've met it. Whatever you're looking for, it is here. I know at least one of these lovely designs will meet your needs and say "make me."

Happy quilting!

Carolyn S. Vagts

Table of Contents

Cottage Scrambler,
page 12

Quilted Roses,
page 29

Woven Indigo

Design by Tricia Lynn Maloney
Quilted by Karen Shields of Karen's Quilting Studio

Fresh white makes a collection of blues "pop." Take traditional colors,
a simple block pattern and create a modern quilt.

Project Specifications
Skill Level: Beginner
Quilt Size: 90" x 90"
Block Size: 9" x 9"
Number of Blocks: 49

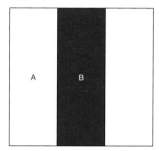

Woven Indigo
9" x 9" Block
Make 49

Materials
- ¼ yard each 13 assorted medium and dark blue prints or tonals
- ¼ yard each 8 assorted blue-and-white prints
- 3⅛ yards medium blue print
- 3⅓ yards white tonal
- Backing 98" x 98"
- Batting 98" x 98"
- Neutral-color all-purpose thread
- Quilting thread
- Basic sewing tools and supplies

Cutting
1. Cut one 3½" by fabric width B strip from each of the 13 assorted medium and dark blue prints or tonals.

2. Cut one 3½" by fabric width strip from each of the eight assorted blue-on-white fabrics; subcut strips into 12 (3½" x 16½") E rectangles, eight 3½" x 9½" F rectangles and four 3½" G squares.

3. Cut eight 9½" by fabric width H/I strips medium blue print.

4. Cut nine 2¼" by fabric width strips medium blue print for binding.

5. Cut 26 (3½" by fabric width) A strips white tonal.

6. Cut seven 2" by fabric width C/D strips white tonal.

Completing the Blocks
1. Select one B strip and two A strips. Sew an A strip to opposite long sides of B to make an A-B strip set; press seams toward B.

2. Subcut the A-B strip set into four 9½" x 9½" Woven Indigo blocks referring to Figure 1.

Figure 1

3. Repeat steps 1 and 2 to make a total of 13 A-B strip sets, then subcutting the strip sets into 49 Woven Indigo blocks.

Completing the Quilt Top

1. Select and join seven assorted Woven Indigo blocks to make an X row referring to Figure 2; press seams toward the upright blocks. Repeat to make a total of four X rows.

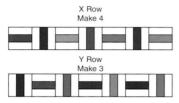

X Row
Make 4

Y Row
Make 3

Figure 2

2. Repeat step 1 to complete three Y rows, again referring to Figure 2.

3. Join the X and Y rows referring to the Placement Diagram to complete the pieced center; press seams in one direction.

4. Join the C/D strips on the short ends to make a long strip; press. Subcut strip into two 2" x 63½" C strips and two 2" x 66½" D strips.

5. Sew C strips to the top and bottom and D strips to opposite sides of the pieced center; press seams toward C and D strips.

6. Select and join three E and two F rectangles to make a side strip referring to Figure 3; press seams in one direction. Repeat to make a second side strip. Sew these strips to opposite sides of the pieced center; press seams toward the D strips.

Figure 3

7. Repeat step 6 and add a G square to each end of each strip; press seams toward G. Sew these strips to the top and bottom of the pieced center; press seams toward C strips.

8. Join the H/I strips on the short ends to make a long strip; press. Subcut strip into two 9½" x 72½" H strips and two 9½" x 90½" I strips.

9. Sew the H strips to the top and bottom, and I strips to opposite sides of the pieced center to complete the quilt top; press seams toward H and I strips.

Completing the Quilt

1. Sandwich the batting between the pieced quilt top and the prepared backing piece; pin or baste layers together to hold. Quilt as desired by hand or machine.

2. When quilting is complete, trim batting and backing fabric even with raw edges of the quilt top.

3. Join binding strips on the short ends to make a long strip; press seams open. Fold the binding strip with wrong sides together along length; press.

4. Sew binding to the quilt edges, mitering corners and overlapping ends. Fold binding to the back side and stitch in place to finish the quilt. ■

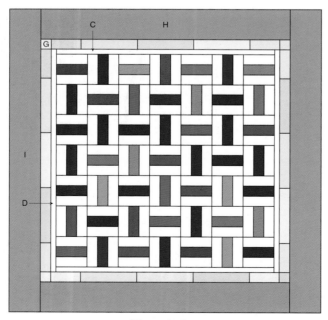

Woven Indigo
Placement Diagram 90" x 90"

"A simple design and gorgeous fabrics were the inspirations for this bed-size quilt. Blue-and-white quilts have been a traditional favorite for a very long time, so this quilt is traditional but with a fresh, modern twist." —Tricia Lynn Maloney

Birch Street

Design by Missy Shepler

Easy piecing and random placement make this a simple quilt to sew in a weekend.

Project Specifications

Skill Level: Confident Beginner
Quilt Size: 48" x 64"
Block Size: 4" x 4"
Number of Blocks: 48

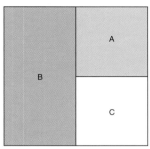

Reversed Colored Birch Street
4" x 4" Block
Make 5

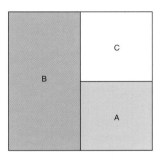

Colored Birch Street
4" x 4" Block
Make 5

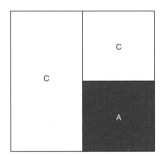

White Birch Street
4" x 4" Block
Make 38

Materials

- 5 fat quarters assorted retro prints
- 3 yards white solid
- Backing 56" x 72"
- Batting 56" x 72"
- Neutral-color all-purpose thread
- Quilting thread
- Basic sewing tools and supplies

Cutting

1. Cut nine 2½" x 21" strips total from the five fat quarters. **Note:** *If any fabric is a directional print, be sure to consider placement of directional objects when cutting pieces or strips.*

2. Subcut the strips cut in step 1 into 48 (2½") A squares and 10 (2½" x 4½") B rectangles.

3. From the remainder of the fat quarters, cut 13 (2¼" x 21") strips to make 236" when joined for binding.

4. Cut eight 2½" by fabric width C strips white solid.

5. Cut 16 (4½" by fabric width) strips; subcut into 144 (4½") D squares.

Completing the Blocks

1. With right sides together, align one raw edge of an A square with the long raw edge of a C strip and stitch the square to the strip.

2. Without removing the strip from beneath the presser foot, align a second A square along the same edge of the C strip, leaving about ¼" between the squares and stitch the square to the strip as shown in Figure 1.

Figure 1

3. Continue adding A squares to the C strip until you run out of C strip.

4. Repeat with remaining A squares and additional C strips until all A squares are sewn to C strips. **Note:** *You should use three whole C strips and perhaps part of a fourth strip for this step.*

5. Press the stitched strips to set the seams, then press seams open.

6. Using a rotary cutter and ruler, trim the C strip even with the A squares to make 48 (2½" x 4½") A-C units referring to Figure 2.

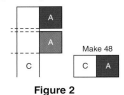

Figure 2

7. Sew B to an A-C unit to complete one Colored Birch Street block referring to Figure 3; press seams open. Repeat to make a total of five blocks and five reverse blocks, again referring to Figure 3.

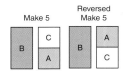

Figure 3

8. With right sides together and aligning raw edges, sew the remaining A-C units to the remaining C strips as in steps 1–5.

9. Using a rotary cutter and ruler, trim the C strip even with the A-C units to complete 38 (4½" x 4½") White Birch Street blocks referring to Figure 4.

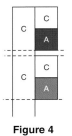

Figure 4

Completing the Top

1. Arrange and join the blocks with the D squares in 16 rows of 12 blocks/squares each, arranging the blocks and squares as desired in each row. Press seams open. **Note:** *Join first in pairs, then join the pairs, and so on to complete the rows.*

2. Join the rows as arranged to complete the quilt top; press seams open.

Completing the Quilt

1. Sandwich the batting between the pieced quilt top and the prepared backing piece; pin or baste layers together to hold. Quilt as desired by hand or machine.

2. When quilting is complete, trim batting and backing fabric even with raw edges of the quilt top.

3. Join binding strips on the short ends to make a long strip; press seams open. Fold the binding strip with wrong sides together along length; press.

4. Sew binding to the quilt edges, mitering corners and overlapping ends. Fold binding to the back side and stitch in place to finish the quilt. ■

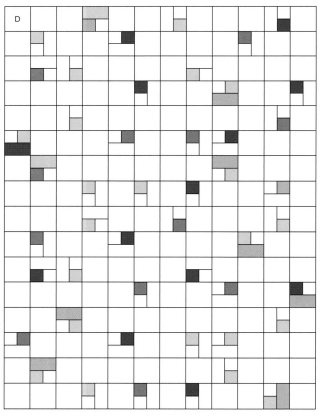

Birch Street
Placement Diagram 48" x 64"

"Five fat quarters of organic cottons given to me by a friend were the inspiration for this quilt. The retro prints remind me of a suburban neighborhood where we lived in ranch houses, drove to work every day, and seemed to live the 'sitcom.' Birch Street quilt echoes that era in an abstract way." —Missy Shepler

Trellised Garden

Design by Chris Malone
Quilted by June Macauley

This garden will last all year long. A little effort, a few fat quarters and some white fabric will produce this garden in a weekend.

Project Specifications
Skill Level: Confident Beginner
Quilt Size: 85" x 102"
Block Size: 8½" x 8½"
Number of Blocks: 120

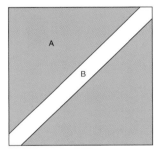

Trellis
8½" x 8½" Block
Make 120

Materials
- 30 fat quarters assorted coordinating pastel prints in rose, lavender, yellow, green and blue
- 1 yard green dot
- 2⅛ yards white tonal
- Backing 93" x 110"
- Batting 93" x 110"
- Neutral-color all-purpose thread
- Quilting thread
- Square ruler 9" x 9" or larger
- Basic sewing tools and supplies

Cutting
1. Cut four (9") squares from each assorted pastel print fat quarters; to total 120 squares; cut each square in half on one diagonal to make 240 A triangles.

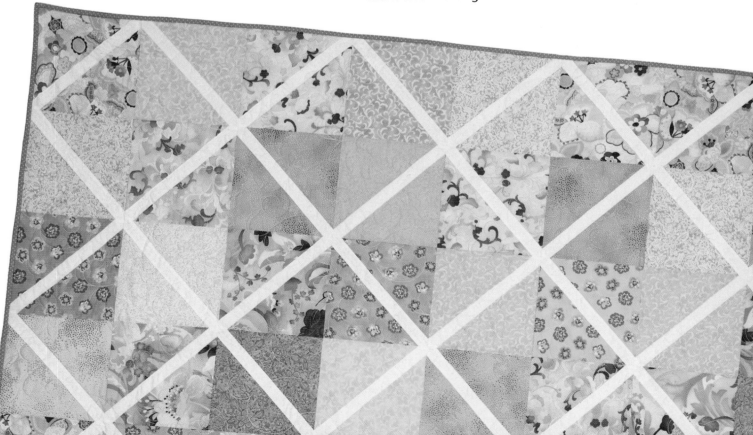

2. Cut five 13" by fabric width strips white tonal; subcut strips into 120 (1½" x 13") B strips.

3. Cut 10 (2¼" by fabric width) strips green dot for binding.

Completing the Blocks

1. Select two same-fabric A triangles and one B strip to complete one Trellis block.

2. Fold each of the selected A triangles in half on the long side on the cut edge and crease to mark the centers as shown in Figure 1.

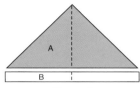

Figure 1

3. Fold the B strip to mark the center, again referring to Figure 1.

4. Matching center marks, sew an A triangle to opposite sides of B as shown in Figure 2.

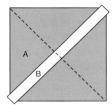

Figure 2

5. Place the block on a cutting mat and align the 45-degree line on the square ruler with the center of the white strip and trim the block to 9" x 9" to complete as shown in Figure 3.

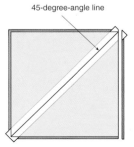

45-degree-angle line

Figure 3

6. Repeat steps 1–5 to complete a total of 120 Trellis blocks.

Completing the Top

1. Arrange and join 10 Trellis blocks to make a row referring to Figure 4; press seams to the right. Repeat to make a total of 12 rows.

Make 12

Figure 4

2. Arrange and join the rows to form the trellis design to complete the quilt top referring to the Placement Diagram for positioning of rows; press seams in one direction.

Completing the Quilt

1. Sandwich the batting between the pieced quilt top and the prepared backing piece; pin or baste layers together to hold. Quilt as desired by hand or machine.

2. When quilting is complete, trim batting and backing fabric even with raw edges of the quilt top.

3. Join binding strips on the short ends to make a long strip; press seams open. Fold the binding strip with wrong sides together along length; press.

4. Sew binding to the quilt edges, mitering corners and overlapping ends. Fold binding to the back side and stitch in place to finish the quilt. ■

Trellised Garden
Placement Diagram 85" x 102"

Cottage Scrambler

Design by Julie Weaver

Take a fun collection and scramble it up into a fantastic throw or lap quilt.

Project Specifications
Skill Level: Confident Beginner
Quilt Size: 50" x 60"
Block Size: 10" x 10"
Number of Blocks: 20

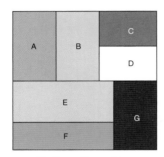

Cottage Scrambler
10" x 10" Block
Make 20

Materials
- ⅜ yard yellow/white print (F)
- ½ yard blue/white floral (A)
- ½ yard black/white print (C)
- ½ yard black weave print (G)
- ½ yard white floral (D)
- ½ yard yellow floral (B)
- ⅝ yard multicolored braid (E)
- 1⅝ yards blue weave print
- Backing 58" x 68"
- Batting 58" x 68"
- Neutral-color all-purpose thread
- Quilting thread
- Basic sewing tools and supplies

Cutting
1. Cut three 3½" by fabric width strips each fabrics A and B.

2. Cut three 3" by fabric width strips each fabrics C and D.

3. Cut four 3½" by fabric width strips fabric E.

4. Cut four 2½" by fabric width strips fabric F.

5. Cut three 3½" by fabric width strips fabric G; subcut strips into 20 (3½" x 5½") G rectangles.

6. Cut two 1½" by fabric width strips each fabrics B, C, D and E. Subcut strips into eight 1½" x 7" rectangles each fabric.

7. Cut five 1½" by fabric width H/I strips blue weave print.

8. Cut six 3½" by fabric width J/K strips blue weave print.

9. Cut six 2¼" by fabric width strips blue weave print for binding.

Completing the Blocks
1. Sew a fabric-width A strip to a B fabric-width strip along length to make an A-B strip set; press. Repeat to make a total of three A-B strip sets.

2. Subcut the A-B strip sets into 20 (5½" x 6½") A-B segments as shown in Figure 1.

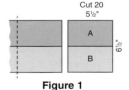

Cut 20
5½"

Figure 1

3. Sew a C fabric-width strip to a D fabric-width strip along length to make a C-D strip set; press. Repeat to make a total of three C-D strip sets.

4. Subcut the C-D strip sets into 20 (4½" x 5½") C-D segments as shown in Figure 2.

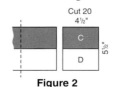

Cut 20
4½"

Figure 2

5. Sew an A-B segment to a C-D segment to make an A row as shown in Figure 3. Repeat to make a total of 20 A rows.

A Row
Make 20

Figure 3

6. Sew a fabric-width E strip to a fabric-width F strip along length to make an E-F strip set; press. Repeat to make a total of four E-F strip sets.

7. Subcut the E-F strip sets into 20 (7½" x 5½") E-F segments referring to Figure 4.

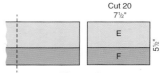

Cut 20
7½"
E
F
5½"

Figure 4

8. Sew a G rectangle to each E-F segment to make 20 G rows as shown in Figure 5.

G Row
Make 20

G

Figure 5

9. To complete one Cottage Scrambler block select and join one each A and G row referring to Figure 6; press.

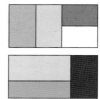

Figure 6

10. Repeat step 9 to make a total of 20 Cottage Scrambler blocks.

Completing the Top

1. Select and join four blocks to make a row, turning every other block referring to Figure 7; press seams in one direction.

Make 5

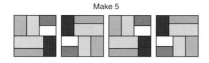

Figure 7

2. Repeat step 1 to make a total of five rows, pressing seams in two rows in one direction and three rows in the opposite direction.

3. Join the rows, alternating seam-pressing directions, to complete the pieced center.

4. Join the H/I strips on the short ends to make a long strip; press. Subcut strip into two 1½" x 50½" H strips and two 1½" x 42½" I strips.

5. Sew the H strips to opposite sides and I strips to the top and bottom of the pieced center.

6. Select and join one 1½" x 7" rectangle from each B, C, D and E fabric to make a rectangle unit referring to Figure 8. Repeat to make eight rectangle units, keeping fabrics in the same order.

Make 8

E   C   D   B

Figure 8

7. Select and join two rectangle units, keeping the same order, to make a border unit. Repeat to make a total of four border units.

8. Sew a border unit to opposite long sides of the pieced center; press seams away from the border units.

9. Center and sew a border unit to the top and bottom of the pieced center; trim excess at each end and press seams away from the border units.

10. Join the J/K strips on the short ends to make a long strip; press. Subcut strip into two 3½" x 54½" J strips and two 3½" x 50½" K strips.

11. Sew the J strips to opposite long sides and the K strips to the top and bottom of the pieced center to complete the quilt top.

Completing the Quilt

1. Sandwich the batting between the pieced quilt top and the prepared backing piece; pin or baste layers together to hold. Quilt as desired by hand or machine.

2. When quilting is complete, trim batting and backing fabric even with raw edges of the quilt top.

3. Join binding strips on the short ends to make a long strip; press seams open. Fold the binding strip with wrong sides together along length; press.

4. Sew binding to the quilt edges, mitering corners and overlapping ends. Fold binding to the back side and stitch in place to finish the quilt. ■

"When I got the fabric I wasn't sure about it because it so isn't me. But the more I worked with the fabrics and saw how the quilt was turning out, I started loving it! The colors are soothing and definitely give a cottage 'feel' to the quilt." —Julie Weaver

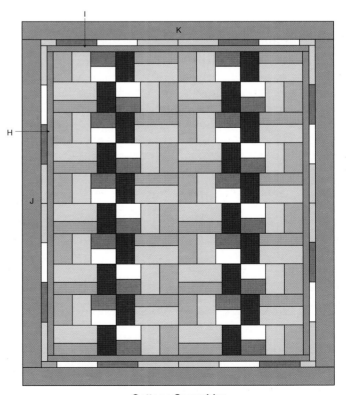

Cottage Scrambler
Placement Diagram 50" x 60"

Straight Stitches

Design by Missy Shepler

Take your favorite fabrics and add long straight-stitch quilting to create a fast and easy lap quilt this weekend.

Project Specifications

Skill Level: Beginner
Quilt Size: 53½" x 48½"

Materials

- ⅝ yard green solid
- 1⅛ yards multiprint
- 1⅛ yards red tonal stripe
- Backing 62" x 57"
- Batting 62" x 57"
- Neutral-color all-purpose thread
- Red and green 12-wt cotton thread
- Walking foot attachment
- Topstitching needle (90/14 or 100/16)
- Basic sewing tools and supplies

Cutting

1. Cut six 2¼" by fabric width strips green solid for binding.

2. Fold the multiprint fabric with selvages together. Square each end of the fabric, trimming as little as necessary referring to Figure 1. Refold the fabric lengthwise so that the cut ends are together, and trim the selvage edges from each edge. Cut carefully so that the corners form a 90-degree angle. Trim the panel to 42" x 37", if necessary.

Figure 1

3. Cut two 6½" x 37" strips along the length of the red tonal stripe for side borders.

4. Cut four 6½" by remaining fabric width strips tonal stripe for top and bottom borders.

Completing the Quilt Top

1. Sew the side border strips to the 37" edges of the trimmed center panel; press seams toward strips.

2. Join two 6½"-wide top/bottom strips on the short ends to make a long strip; press seam open. Trim strip to 54" to make the top strip. Repeat to make the bottom strip. Sew these strips to the top and bottom of the bordered panel to complete the quilt top.

Completing the Quilt

1. Sandwich the batting between the completed quilt top and the prepared backing piece; pin or baste layers together to hold.

2. Mark a line 3" from the left-side border seam toward the center of the quilt as shown in Figure 2; draw another line 4" from the first marked line. Continue to mark three more lines 4" apart. Repeat to mark lines from the right-side border seam. *Note: The drawing colors are faded throughout this section to better show the marked and stitched lines.*

Figure 2

3. Insert the topstitching needle in your machine and set the machine for a long stitch length. Using a walking foot and the red 12-wt thread, machine-stitch on marked lines, keeping stitching as straight as possible.

4. Continuing to use red thread, sew lines of stitching ½" to the right and left of the stitched lines as shown in Figure 3.

Figure 3

5. Mark a line ¼" from the side seam on the left border as shown in Figure 4; mark a second line 4" from the first. Repeat on the right border.

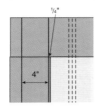

Figure 4

6. With red thread, stitch on the marked lines and ½" on each side of the marked lines as shown in Figure 5.

Figure 5

7. Change to green 12-wt cotton thread and stitch between the stitched red lines referring to Figure 6 to complete the stitching.

Figure 6

8. Trim batting and backing even with the edges of the quilted top.

9. Join binding strips on the short ends to make a long strip; press seams open. Fold the binding strip with wrong sides together along length; press.

10. Sew binding to the quilt edges, mitering corners and overlapping ends. Fold binding to the back side and stitch in place to finish the quilt. ■

"Feature two favorite fabrics in this super-simple quilt. The center panel is perfect for displaying yardage that you just don't want to cut into pieces, and easy quilting lines ensure that it'll be done by Monday." —Missy Shepler

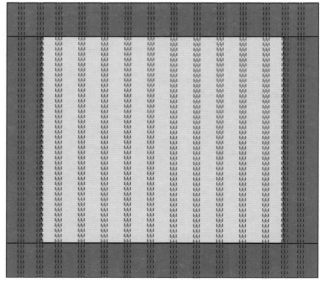

Straight Stitches
Placement Diagram 53½" x 48½"

Square It Up

Design by Chris Malone
Quilted by June Macauley

This quilt provides a great way to play with a scrappy layout.
Just pick a strip and go with it!

Project Specifications
Skill Level: Confident Beginner
Quilt Size: 80" x 90"
Block Size: 10" x 10"
Number of Blocks: 72

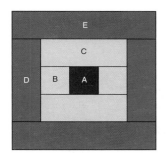

Dark-Bordered Square
10" x 10" Block
Make 36

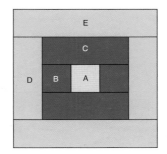

Light-Bordered Square
10" x 10" Block
Make 36

Materials
• 117 precut 2½" by fabric width strips assorted blue, green and purple prints in light, medium and dark values
• Backing 88" x 98"
• Batting 88" x 98"
• Neutral-color all-purpose thread
• Quilting thread
• Basic sewing tools and supplies

Cutting
1. Sort the assorted fabric strips into two groups—dark/medium (dark) and light/medium (light). Pull nine strips for the binding. The remaining assortments of dark and light strips should be equal in number.

2. Cut the following from the dark strips: 36 (2½") A squares for block centers, 36 sets of two 2½" B squares and two 2½" x 6½" C strips (each set from the same print), and 36 sets of two 2½" x 6½" D and two 2½" x 10½" E strips (each set from the same print). ***Note:*** *For maximum yield, from a single strip*

cut two D strips and two E strips; reserve remaining scrap. Cut four 2½" B squares and four C strips from a single strip; reserve scrap. Cut the A squares from the reserved scraps.

3. Repeat step 2 with the light strips.

Completing the Blocks

1. To complete a Dark-Bordered Square block, select a matching set of light B squares and C strips, a matching set of dark D and E strips, and a different-fabric dark A square.

2. Sew a B square to opposite sides of the A square; press seams toward B. Sew a C strip to the top and bottom of the A-B unit as shown in Figure 1; press seams toward C.

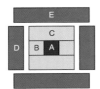

Figure 1

3. Sew a D strip to the B sides of the A-B-C unit and an E strip to the C sides to complete one Dark-Bordered Square block, again referring to Figure 1.

4. Repeat steps 1–3 to complete a total of 36 Dark-Bordered Square blocks.

5. To complete a Light-Bordered Square block, select a matching set of dark B squares and C strips, a matching set of light D and E strips, and a different-fabric light A square.

6. Repeat steps 2 and 3 to complete one Light-Bordered Square block referring to Figure 2.

Figure 2

7. Repeat steps 5 and 6 to complete a total of 36 Light-Bordered Square blocks.

Completing the Top

1. Select and join four each Light- and Dark-Bordered Square blocks, turning every other block referring to Figure 3 to make a row; press seams toward Dark-Bordered Square blocks. Repeat to make nine rows.

Make 9

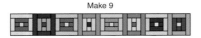

Figure 3

2. Arrange and join the rows, turning every other row referring to the Placement Diagram, to complete the pieced top; press seams in one direction.

Completing the Quilt

1. Sandwich the batting between the pieced quilt top and the prepared backing piece; pin or baste layers together to hold. Quilt as desired by hand or machine.

2. When quilting is complete, trim batting and backing fabric even with raw edges of the quilt top.

3. Join binding strips on the short ends to make a long strip; press seams open. Fold the binding strip with wrong sides together along length; press.

4. Sew binding to the quilt edges, mitering corners and overlapping ends. Fold binding to the back side and stitch in place to finish the quilt. ■

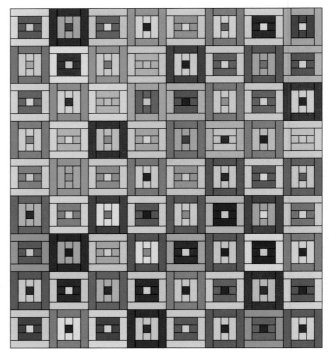

Square It Up
Placement Diagram 80" x 90"

Twister Wall Hanging

Design by Julie Weaver

Add a twist of style to any wall this weekend. The twisted borders around the center blocks give the illusion of dimension to this wall hanging.

Project Specifications
Skill Level: Intermediate
Wall Hanging Size: 36" x 36"
Block Size: 6" x 6"
Number of Blocks: 4

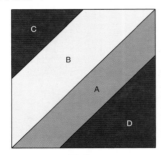

Twist
6" x 6" Block
Make 4

Materials
- ⅓ yard light green batik
- ⅞ yard green leaf batik
- 1 yard cream batik
- 1⅛ yards dark green batik
- Backing 44" x 44"
- Batting 44" x 44"
- Neutral-color all-purpose thread
- Quilting thread
- Basic sewing tools and supplies

Cutting
1. Cut one 6⅞" by fabric width strip light green batik; subcut strip into two 6⅞" A squares.

2. Cut two 3½" by fabric width strips green leaf batik; subcut strips into four 3½" C squares and eight 3½" x 6½" F rectangles.

3. Cut four 4½" by fabric width strips green leaf batik; subcut strips into eight 4½" D squares and 36 (2½" x 4½") O rectangles.

4. Cut one 6⅞" by fabric width strip cream batik; subcut strip into two 6⅞" B squares.

5. Cut three 3½" by fabric width strips cream batik; subcut strips into four rectangles each 3½" x 9½" J and 3½" x 12½" K.

6. Cut two 4½" by fabric width strips cream batik; subcut strips into 32 (1½" x 4½") N rectangles.

7. Cut two 3½" by fabric width strips dark green batik; subcut strips into two 3½" E squares and two rectangles each 3½" x 9½" G, 3½" x 12½" H and 3½" x 6½" I.

8. Cut eight 1½" by fabric width strips dark green batik; trim strips to make two strips each as follows: 1½" x 24½" L, 1½" x 26½" M, 1½" x 34½" P and 1½" x 36½" Q strips.

9. Cut four 2¼" by fabric width dark green batik for binding.

Completing the Blocks
1. Mark a diagonal line from corner to corner on the wrong side of each B, C and four D squares.

2. Place a B square right sides together with an A square and stitch ¼" on each side of the marked line referring to Figure 1.

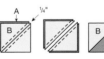

Figure 1

3. Cut apart on the marked line and press open with seams toward A to complete two A-B units, again referring to Figure 1.

4. Place a C square on the B corner and a D square on the A corner of the A-B units and stitch on the marked lines as shown in Figure 2; trim seams to ¼" and press C and D to the right side to complete two Twist blocks, again referring to Figure 2.

Figure 2

5. Repeat steps 2–4 to complete a total of four Twist blocks.

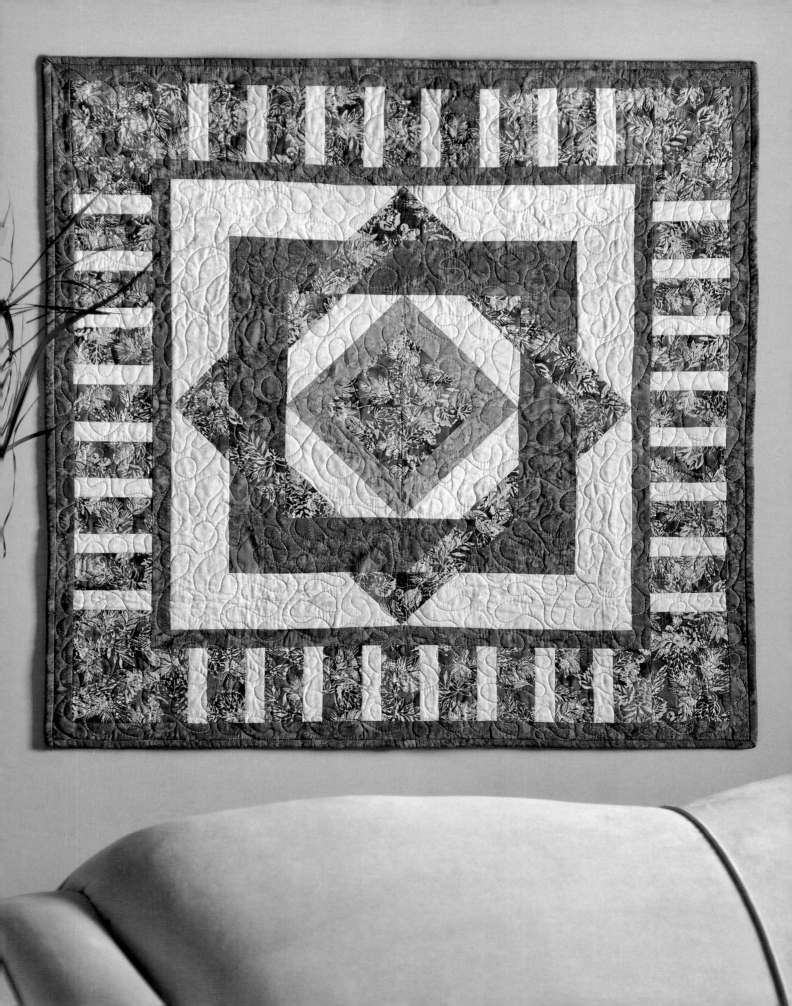

Completing the Top

1. Arrange and join the four Twist blocks to complete the quilt center referring to Figure 3.

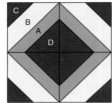

Figure 3

2. Draw a diagonal line from corner to corner on the wrong side of the E squares.

3. Place a marked E square right sides together on the left end of an F rectangle and stitch on the marked line as shown in Figure 4; trim seam to ¼" and press E to the right side.

Figure 4

4. Place a G rectangle right sides together on the opposite end of the E-F unit at a 90-degree angle as shown in Figure 5. Measure 3½" over from the bottom corner of G and draw a line from that point to the top corner; stitch on the marked line. Trim seam to ¼" and press G to the right side to complete an E-F-G unit as shown in Figure 5.

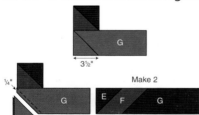

Figure 5

5. Repeat steps 3 and 4 to make a second E-F-G unit.

6. Sew an E-F-G unit to opposite sides of the pieced center referring to Figure 6.

Figure 6

7. Place an I rectangle on the left end of an F rectangle at a 90-degree angle as shown in Figure 7; measure down 3½" from the top raw edge of I and

mark. Draw a diagonal line from the mark to the top right corner and stitch on the marked line as shown in Figure 7; trim seam to ¼" and press I to the right side to complete the F-I unit, again referring to Figure 7.

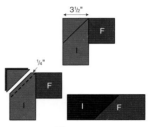

Figure 7

8. Repeat step 7 with H on the F end of an F-I unit referring to Figure 8 to complete an H-F-I unit.

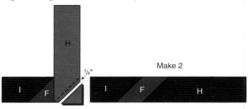

Figure 8

9. Repeat steps 7 and 8 to make a second H-F-I unit. Sew these units to the top and bottom of the pieced center referring to Figure 9; press seams toward the units.

Figure 9

10. Place a J rectangle right sides together on the left end of an F rectangle at a 90-degree angle; measure, mark, stitch and trim as in step 7 and referring to Figure 10. Press seam toward F.

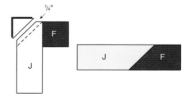

Figure 10

11. Repeat step 10 on the opposite end of F to complete an F-J unit as shown in Figure 11. Repeat to make a second unit.

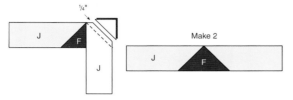

Figure 11

12. Sew the F-J units to opposite sides of the pieced center; press seams toward the F-J units as shown in Figure 12.

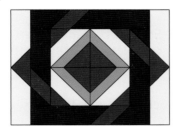

Figure 12

13. Repeat steps 10 and 11 with F and K pieces to make F-K units and sew to the top and bottom of the pieced center referring to Figure 13.

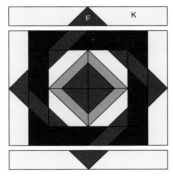

Figure 13

14. Sew L strips to opposite sides and M strips to the top and bottom of the pieced center; press seams toward L and M strips.

15. Select and join eight N rectangles and nine O rectangles to make a pieced strip as shown in Figure 14; press seams toward O. Repeat to make four pieced strips.

Figure 14

16. Sew a pieced strip to opposite sides of the pieced center; press seams toward L strips.

17. Sew a D square to each end of each remaining pieced strip and sew to the top and bottom of the pieced center; press seams toward D and then toward M.

18. Sew P strips to opposite sides and Q strips to the top and bottom of the pieced center; press seams toward P and Q strips.

Completing the Quilt

1. Sandwich the batting between the pieced top and the prepared backing piece; pin or baste layers together to hold. Quilt as desired by hand or machine.

2. When quilting is complete, trim batting and backing fabric even with raw edges of the wall hanging top.

3. Join binding strips on the short ends to make a long strip; press seams open. Fold the binding strip with wrong sides together along length; press.

4. Sew binding to the wall hanging edges, mitering corners and overlapping ends. Fold binding to the back side and stitch in place to finish the wall hanging. ∎

"I like the challenge of nontraditional piecing. I think the 'non' use of half-square triangles, Flying Geese, etc., is definitely that. I am beginning to really like batik fabrics, so both the fabric and the piecing challenged and inspired me on this one." —Julie Weaver

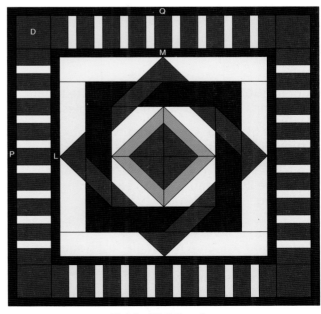

Twister Wall Hanging
Placement Diagram 36" x 36"

Stacked Blocks

Design by Gina Gempesaw
Machine-Quilted by Carole Whaling

Make a fun and stylish quilt with 10" squares and a background fabric—
one day to piece and one day to quilt—and it's done by Monday!

Project Specifications
Skill Level: Beginner
Quilt Size: 81" x 95½"
Block Size: 14" x 9½"
Number of Blocks: 36

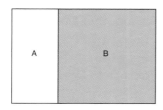

Stacked
14" x 9½" Block
Make 36

Materials
- 36 (10") precut B squares prints, solids or tonals
- ¾ yard orange batik
- 4 yards white tonal
- Backing 89" x 104"
- Batting 89" x 104"
- Neutral-color all-purpose thread
- Quilting thread
- Basic sewing tools and supplies

Cutting
1. Cut five 10" by fabric width strips white tonal; subcut strips into 36 (5" x 10") A rectangles.

2. Cut five 5½" x 86" C strips and two 5½" x 81½" D strips along the remaining length of the white tonal.

3. Cut nine 2¼" by fabric width strips orange batik for binding.

Completing the Blocks
1. Select and sew an A rectangle to a B square to complete one Stacked block referring to the block drawing; press seam toward B.

2. Repeat step 1 to complete a total of 36 Stacked blocks.

Completing the Quilt Top
1. Select nine Stacked blocks and join referring to Figure 1 to complete 1 block strip; press seams in one direction. Repeat to make a total of four block strips.

2. Join the block strips with the C strips referring to the Placement Diagram; press seams toward C strips.

Make 4

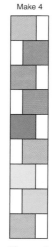

Figure 1

3. Sew D strips to the top and bottom of the pieced section to complete the quilt top; press seams toward D strips.

Completing the Quilt
1. Sandwich the batting between the pieced quilt top and the prepared backing piece; pin or baste layers together to hold. Quilt as desired by hand or machine.

2. When quilting is complete, trim batting and backing fabric even with raw edges of the quilt top.

3. Join binding strips on the short ends to make a long strip; press seams open. Fold the binding strip with wrong sides together along length; press.

4. Sew binding to the quilt edges, mitering corners and overlapping ends. Fold binding to the back side and stitch in place to finish the quilt. ▪

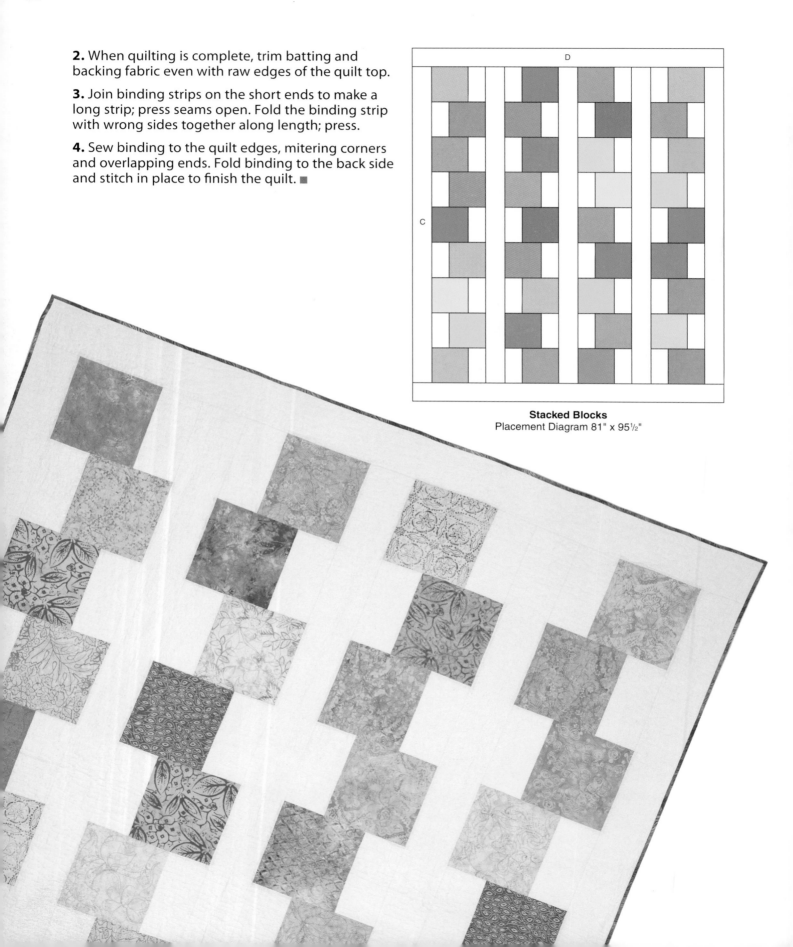

Stacked Blocks
Placement Diagram 81" x 95½"

Quilted Roses

Design by Bev Remillard for Ladylike Designs

This machine fusible appliqué can be done in a weekend if you're an overachiever.

Project Specifications
Skill Level: Advanced
Quilt Size: 48" x 48"
Block Size: 12" x 12"
Number of Blocks: 9

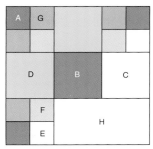

Nine-Patch
12" x 12" Block
Make 4

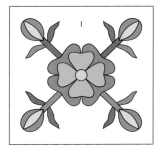

Rose
12" x 12" Block
Make 5

Materials
- 1 fat eighth each 3 medium green tonals
- ⅜ yard light yellow tonal
- ½ yard total bright aqua prints
- 1¼ yards cream print
- 1⅜ yards peach/cream print
- 1⅜ yards total salmon florals
- Backing 56" x 56"
- Batting 56" x 56"
- Cream all-purpose thread
- Quilting thread
- 1¼ yards 18"-wide fusible web
- 2 yards 20"-wide fabric stabilizer
- Basic sewing tools and supplies

Cutting

1. Cut two 2½" by fabric width G strips bright aqua print.

2. Cut one 1½" by fabric width strip bright aqua print; subcut strip into four 1½" K squares.

3. Cut one 4½" by fabric width strip light yellow tonal; subcut strip into eight 4½" D squares.

4. Cut one 4½" by fabric width strip salmon floral; subcut strip into four 4½" B squares.

5. Cut two 1½" x 38½" L strips and two 1½" x 40½" M strips salmon floral.

6. Cut five 2¼" by fabric width strips salmon floral for binding.

7. Cut one 2½" by fabric width A strip salmon floral.

8. Cut two 4½" by fabric width strips cream print; subcut strips into four 4½" C squares and four 4½" x 8½" H rectangles.

9. Cut one 2½" by fabric width E strip cream print.

10. Cut two 13" by fabric width strips cream print; subcut strips into five 13" I squares.

11. Cut two 2½" by fabric width F strips peach/cream print.

12. Cut one 12½" by fabric width strip peach/cream print; subcut strip into 12 (1½" x 12½") J strips.

13. Cut five 4½" by fabric width N strips peach/cream print.

14. Cut five 13" squares fabric stabilizer.

Cutting the Appliqué Pieces

1. Trace appliqué shapes given onto the paper side of the fusible web as directed on individual pattern pieces and leaving ¼" between pieces.

2. Cut out shapes leaving a margin around each one.

3. Fuse shapes to the wrong side of fabrics as directed on pattern for color and number to cut. Cut out shapes on traced lines. Remove paper backing.

Completing the Nine-Patch Blocks

1. Sew the A strip to a G strip along length to make an A-G strip set; press seam toward G.

2. Subcut the A-G strip set into 12 (2½" x 4½") A-G units as shown in Figure 1.

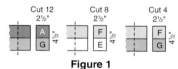

Figure 1

3. Repeat step 1 with E and F strips and subcut into eight 2½" x 4½" E-F units, again referring to Figure 1.

4. Repeat step 1 with F and G strips and subcut into four 2½" x 4½" F-G units, again referring to Figure 1.

5. Arrange and join the A-G, E-F and F-G units to make four of each combination of corner units referring to Figure 2 for positioning of units; press.

Figure 2

6. To make one Nine-Patch block, select one A-G-F-G corner unit, two A-G-E-F corner units, one each B and C square, two D squares and one H rectangle.

7. Arrange and join the pieces/units from step 6 in rows referring to Figure 3; press seams toward D and H and away from B in the center row. Join the rows to complete one Nine-Patch block.

Figure 3

9. Repeat steps 6 and 7 to complete a total of four Nine-Patch blocks.

Completing the Rose Blocks

1. Fold and crease the I squares to mark the horizontal, vertical and diagonal centers as shown in Figure 4.

Figure 4

2. Select four each leaves, reverse leaves, buds, bud centers, stems, large petals and small petals and one flower center.

3. Arrange and fuse the appliqué shapes in numerical order on an I square referring to Figure 5 and the pattern given.

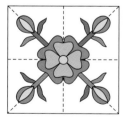

Figure 5

4. Repeat steps 2 and 3 to fuse a total of five Rose blocks.

5. Pin fabric stabilizer to the wrong side of each Rose block.

6. Using cream thread and a narrow buttonhole stitch, sew around each fused shape on all Rose blocks.

7. Trim each Rose block to 12½" x 12½", centering motif.

8. When all stitching is complete, remove fabric stabilizer.

Completing the Quilt Top

1. Arrange and join one Rose block with two Nine-Patch blocks and two J strips to make an X row as shown in Figure 6; press seams toward J strips. Repeat to make a total of two X rows.

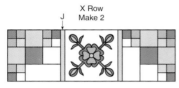

Figure 6

2. Arrange and join three Rose blocks with two J strips to make the center row referring to Figure 7; press seams toward J strips.

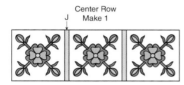

Figure 7

3. Join three J strips with two K squares to make a sashing row; press seams toward J strips. Repeat to make a second sashing row.

4. Sew a sashing row to opposite sides of the center row and add an X row to the remaining side of each sashing row to complete the pieced center; press seams toward the sashing rows.

5. Sew L strips to the top and bottom, and M strips to opposite sides of the pieced center; press seams toward L and M strips.

6. Join the N strips on short ends to make a long strip; press seams open. Subcut strip into four 4½" x 52" N strips.

7. Center and sew an N strip to each side of the bordered center, beginning and ending stitching ¼" from each corner as shown in Figure 8.

Figure 8

8. Fold the quilt top in half diagonally with wrong sides together. Place the ends of two borders right sides together and pin to hold. Align the 45-degree-angle line of a rotary-cutting ruler on the border seam line. Mark a line from the end of the stitching line to the outer edge of the layered border strip ends referring to Figure 9.

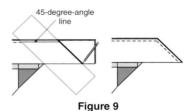

Figure 9

9. Stitch on the marked line. Trim ¼" beyond the stitched line, again referring to Figure 9. Unfold the quilt top. Press the mitered corner seam open to finish.

Completing the Quilt

1. Sandwich the batting between the pieced quilt top and the prepared backing piece; pin or baste layers together to hold. Quilt as desired by hand or machine.

2. When quilting is complete, trim batting and backing fabric even with raw edges of the quilt top.

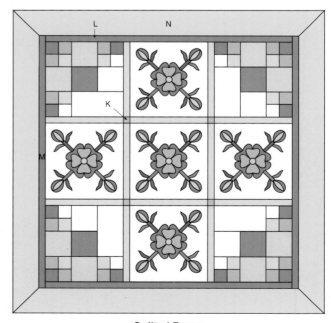

Quilted Roses
Placement Diagram 48" x 48"

3. Join binding strips on the short ends to make a long strip; press seams open. Fold the binding strip with wrong sides together along length; press.

4. Sew binding to the quilt edges, mitering corners and overlapping ends. Fold binding to the back side and stitch in place to finish the quilt. ■

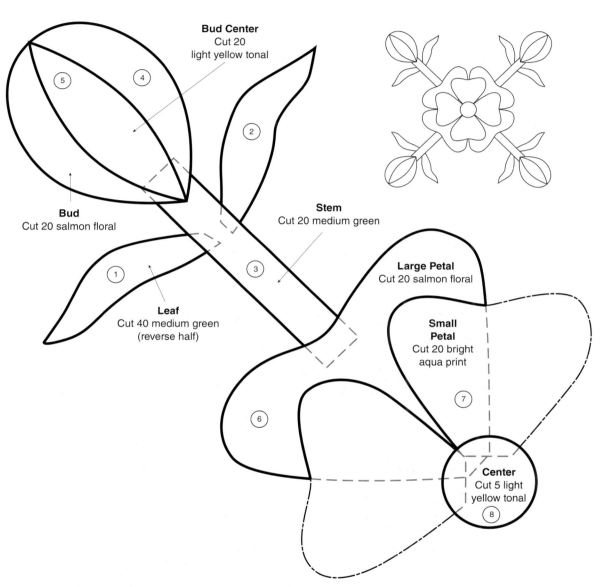

Bud Center
Cut 20
light yellow tonal

Bud
Cut 20 salmon floral

Stem
Cut 20 medium green

Large Petal
Cut 20 salmon floral

Small Petal
Cut 20 bright aqua print

Leaf
Cut 40 medium green
(reverse half)

Center
Cut 5 light yellow tonal

Quilted Roses ¼ Appliqué Pattern

Strip Dash Runner

Design by Tricia Lynn Maloney

Transform your bed or table in a weekend with this super-simple runner made out of sumptuous Bali batik precuts. Precut strips make this a fast and easy weekend project.

Project Specifications
Skill Level: Beginner
Bed Runner Size: 90" x 22"

Materials
- 45 precut 2½" x 15½" batik A strips
- ⅝ yard brown batik
- ¾ yard light blue-green batik
- Backing 98" x 30"
- Batting 98" x 30"
- Neutral-color all-purpose thread
- Quilting thread
- Basic sewing tools and supplies

Cutting
1. Cut six 2¼" by fabric width strips brown batik for binding.

2. Cut three 7½" by fabric width strips light blue-green batik; subcut strips into 45 (2½" x 7½") B strips.

Completing the Top
1. Sew a B strip to an A strip to make an A-B unit as shown in Figure 1; press.

Figure 1

2. Repeat step 1 to make a total of 45 A-B units.

3. Select two different A-B units and join to make a strip unit, alternating the orientation of the pieces as shown in Figure 2. Repeat to make 22 strip units.

Make 22

Figure 2

4. Join two strip units to make an A-B quad unit as shown in Figure 3. Repeat to make 11 quad units.

Make 11

Figure 3

5. Join the quad units and add the extra A-B unit to one end to complete the pieced top.

Completing the Quilt

1. Sandwich the batting between the pieced bed runner top and the prepared backing piece; pin or baste layers together to hold. Quilt as desired by hand or machine.

2. When quilting is complete, trim batting and backing fabric even with raw edges of the bed runner top.

3. Join binding strips on the short ends to make a long strip; press seams open. Fold the binding strip with wrong sides together along length; press.

4. Sew binding to the bed runner edges, mitering corners and overlapping ends. Fold binding to the back side and stitch in place to finish the bed runner. ■

"I really enjoy the challenge of designing projects using precut fabrics, and who can go wrong with a yummy collection of batiks?" –Tricia Lynn Maloney

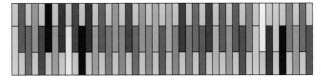

Strip Dash Bed Runner
Placement Diagram 90" x 22"

Abundance Place Mats

Design by Sandra L. Hatch

Create wonderful place mats and table toppers from panels. The possibilities are endless when you consider all the panels available.

Specifications
Skill Level: Beginner
Place Mat Size: 19" x 19"

Materials
- Materials listed will make 2 place mats.
- 2 panels at least 8¾" square
- 1 fat quarter small black print
- ½ yard large black print
- ⅞ yard cream print
- 1⅝ yards backing fabric
- 2 squares batting 25" x 25"
- Black all-purpose thread
- Basic sewing tools and supplies

Cutting
1. Trim panels to make two (8¾") A squares, centering the motifs. ***Note:*** *See Adjusting Panel Size for more information.*

2. Cut two 4¾" x 21" strips small black print; subcut strips into six 4¾" squares. Cut each square on both diagonals to make 24 D1 triangles.

3. Cut four 3" by fabric width strips large black print; subcut strips into four 3" x 14½" F strips and four 3" x 19½" G strips.

4. Cut three 1¾" by fabric width strips cream print; subcut strips into four 1¾" x 8¾" B strips and four 1¾" x 11" C strips.

5. Cut one 4¾" by fabric width strip cream print; subcut strip into four 4¾" squares. Cut each square on both diagonals to make 16 D2 triangles.

6. Trim the remainder of the strip from step 5 to 4⅜" and subcut into four 4⅜" squares. Cut each of these squares in half on one diagonal to make eight E triangles.

7. Cut five 2¼" by fabric width strips cream print for binding.

8. Cut two 25" squares backing fabric.

Completing the Place Mats
1. Sew a B strip to opposite sides and C strips to the top and bottom of the A panel. Press seams toward strips. Trim the bordered panel to 11" square, centering the panel design.

2. Join three D1 and two D2 triangles to make a side strip referring to Figure 1. Repeat to make four side strips.

Make 4

Figure 1

3. Center and sew a side strip to each side of the bordered A square.

4. Sew an E triangle to each corner of the pieced center.

38

5. Sew an F strip to opposite sides and G strips to the top and bottom of the pieced center to complete the place mat top.

6. Repeat steps 1–5 to complete a second place mat top.

Tip

Adjusting Panel Size

Panels are not all created equal. Even panels of the same design sometimes are not square or perfect in size. This makes it hard to use them in quilts when the math has to work!

Do not fear! It is possible to adjust the size to fit. In the samples shown, the bordered center panel needs to finish at 10½". The center A panel is close to 8¾" square, but not exact on any of the printed lines on the panel. To make sure the bordered A panel works with the pieced borders, a wider-than-needed border is added to each side of the A panel. Then the bordered A panel is trimmed to 11", the size needed to complete this project.

This method of bordering a panel with extra-wide strips and then trimming them works for almost any panel. The trick is to center the panel when trimming.

This is easy to do if you fold the bordered panel in half through the horizontal center of the motif, divide the size needed (don't forget to add the seam allowance!) in half and then trim the folded panel on the raw-edge sides. Repeat this process, folding on the vertical center to make a perfect-size center. The borders may be a little uneven in size, but the bordered panel will be the perfect size for use in your project.

7. For each place mat, sandwich a batting square between a place mat top and a prepared backing piece; pin or baste layers together to hold. Quilt as desired by hand or machine.

8. When quilting is complete, trim batting and backing fabric even with raw edges of each place mat top.

9. Join binding strips on the short ends to make a long strip; press seams open. Fold the binding strip with wrong sides together along length; press.

10. Sew binding to the place mat edges, mitering corners and overlapping ends. Fold binding to the back side and stitch in place to finish the place mats. ■

"Panels are fun to work with and often have really nice designs. Usually they are not printed exactly square, and I like to find creative ways to size them and use them in projects. The colors in these Abundance panels are so rich and make perfect centers for autumn projects." —Sandra L. Hatch

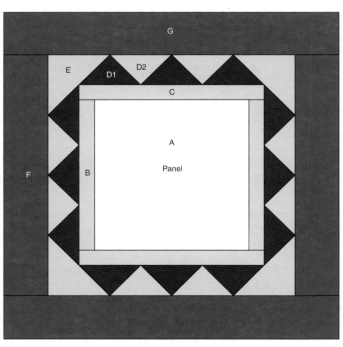

Abundance Place Mat
Placement Diagram 19" x 19"

Happy Hexagons

Design by Sandra L. Hatch

Make this mat as a focal point for your table or add more hexagons to make a dramatic tablecloth.

Specifications
Skill Level: Intermediate
Table Mat Size: Approximately 17½" x 17"
Block Size: 5⅞" x 6⅞"
Number of Blocks: 7

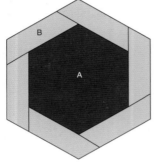

Hexagon
5⅞" x 6⅞" Block
Make 7

Materials
- 7 (5") squares total light and dark brown batiks
- 7 (1½" x 42") strips total light and dark brown batiks
- ½ yard brown batik
- Backing 23" x 24"
- Batting 23" x 24"
- Brown all-purpose thread
- Template material
- Basic sewing tools and supplies

Cutting
1. Prepare a template for the A hexagon using the pattern given. Cut as directed from the 5" batik squares.

2. Cut each 1½" x 42" strip into six (1½" x 4¾") B strips.

3. Prepare 2¼" bias binding strips to total 100" from the ½ yard brown batik.

Completing the Hexagon Blocks
1. To make one Hexagon block, select one dark A hexagon and six light matching B strips.

2. Place a B strip right sides together on one side of A, extending the left end at least 1¾" as shown in Figure 1.

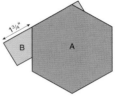

Figure 1

3. Start stitching at least 1" from the left end of the A hexagon to create a partial seam as shown in Figure 2.

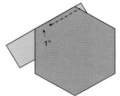

Figure 2

Tip

Die-Cutting Hexagons
Hexagons can be cut easily and accurately when using a die-cutting system such as AccuQuilt's Go! Baby Fabric Cutter and a hexagon die. Every hexagon is the perfect size and you can cut multiples in a jiffy either using scraps or folded fabric yardage.

4. Press the B strip to the right side and trim the short end even with A as shown in Figure 3.

Figure 3

5. Add a second B strip to A referring to Figure 4; press and trim excess B even with A on each end.

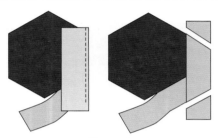

Figure 4

6. Continue to add B strips to A in a counterclockwise direction, trimming and pressing after each addition, until you have added a strip to each side. Now finish the partial seam. Press and trim excess at the end of the partial seam if necessary to complete one Hexagon block.

7. Repeat steps 1–5 to complete a total of 7 Hexagon blocks.

Completing the Table Mat

1. Join the hexagon blocks on ends to make two rows with two blocks and one row with three blocks, stopping stitching ¼" from ends as shown in Figure 5.

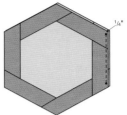

Figure 5

2. Join the rows, stitching from the ends of the stopped seam allowances to make set-in seams. Sew seams at edges all the way to the end of the pieces.

3. Sandwich the batting between the pieced top and the prepared backing piece; pin or baste layers together to hold. Quilt as desired by hand or machine.

4. When quilting is complete, trim batting and backing fabric even with raw edges of the pieced top.

5. Join binding strips on the short ends to make a long strip; press seams open. Fold the binding strip with wrong sides together along length; press.

6. Sew binding to the edges, mitering corners and overlapping ends. Fold binding to the back side and stitch in place to finish. ■

Tip

Binding

Because this project has inverted angles as well as extended angles at the edges, the binding needs to be able to stretch. Straight-of-grain binding is not recommended for this project. Bias binding is preferred.

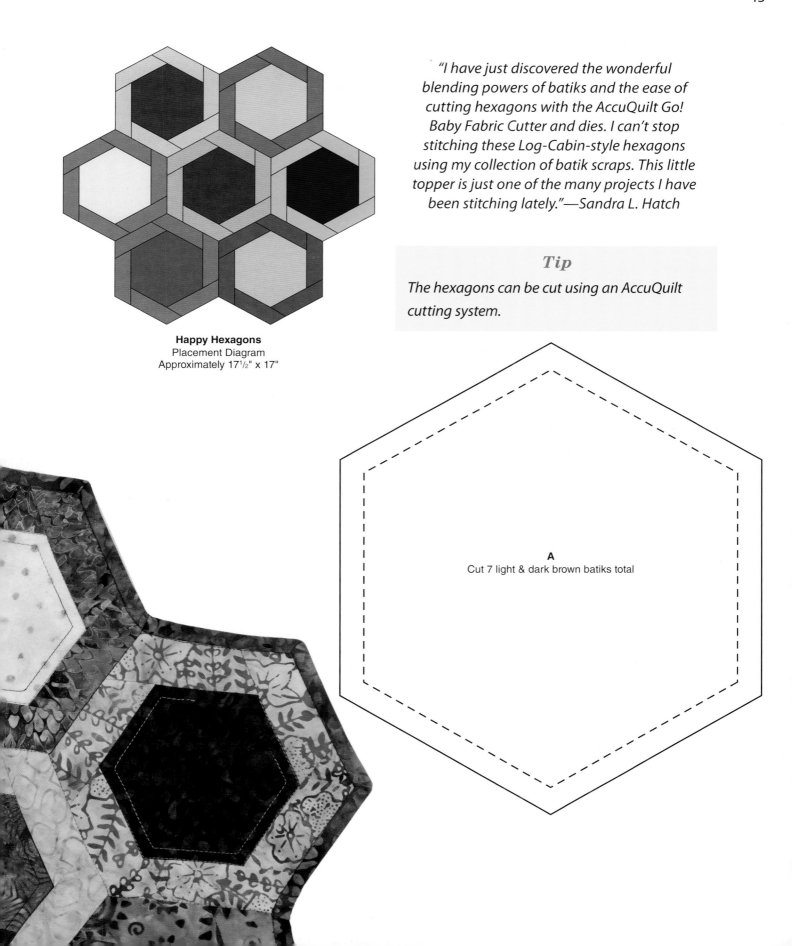

Happy Hexagons
Placement Diagram
Approximately 17½" x 17"

"I have just discovered the wonderful blending powers of batiks and the ease of cutting hexagons with the AccuQuilt Go! Baby Fabric Cutter and dies. I can't stop stitching these Log-Cabin-style hexagons using my collection of batik scraps. This little topper is just one of the many projects I have been stitching lately."—Sandra L. Hatch

Tip

The hexagons can be cut using an AccuQuilt cutting system.

A
Cut 7 light & dark brown batiks total

Quilting Basics

The following is a reference guide. For more information, consult a comprehensive quilting book.

Always:
- Read through the entire pattern before you begin your project.
- Purchase quality, 100 percent cotton fabrics.
- When considering prewashing, do so with ALL of the fabrics being used. Generally, prewashing is not required in quilting.
- Use ¼" seam allowance for all stitching unless otherwise instructed.
- Use a short-to-medium stitch length.
- Make sure your seams are accurate.

Quilting Tools & Supplies
- Rotary cutter and mat
- Scissors for paper and fabric
- Non-slip quilting rulers
- Marking tools
- Sewing machine
- Sewing machine feet:
    ¼" seaming foot (for piecing)
    Walking or even-feed foot (for piecing or quilting)
    Darning or free-motion foot (for free-motion quilting)
- Quilting hand-sewing needles
- Straight pins
- Curved safety pins for basting
- Seam ripper
- Iron and ironing surface

Basic Techniques

Appliqué
Fusible Appliqué
All templates in this book are reversed for use with this technique.

1. Trace the instructed number of templates ¼" apart onto the paper side of paper-backed fusible web. Cut apart the templates, leaving a margin around each, and fuse to the wrong side of the fabric following fusible web manufacturer's instructions.

2. Cut the appliqué pieces out on the traced lines, remove paper backing and fuse to the background referring to the appliqué motif given.

3. Finish appliqué raw edges with a straight, satin, blanket, zigzag or blind-hem machine stitch with matching or invisible thread.

Turned-Edge Appliqué
1. Trace the printed reversed templates onto template plastic. Flip the template over and mark as the right side.

2. Position the template, right side up, on the right side of fabric and lightly trace, spacing images ½" apart. Cut apart, leaving a ¼" margin around the traced lines.

3. Clip curves and press edges ¼" to the wrong side around the appliqué shape.

4. Referring to the appliqué motif, pin or baste appliqué shapes to the background.

5. Hand-stitch shapes in place using a blind stitch and thread to match or machine-stitch using a short blind hemstitch and either matching or invisible thread.

Borders
Most patterns in this book give an exact size to cut borders. You may check those sizes by comparing them to the horizontal and vertical center measurements of your quilt top.

Straight Borders
1. Mark the centers of the side borders and quilt top sides.

2. Stitch borders to quilt top sides with right sides together and matching raw edges and center marks using a ¼" seam. Press seams toward borders.

3. Repeat with top and bottom border lengths.

Mitered Borders
1. Add at least twice the border width to the border lengths instructed to cut.

2. Center and sew the side borders to the quilt, beginning and ending stitching ¼" from the quilt corner and backstitching (Figure 1). Repeat with the top and bottom borders.

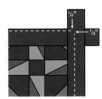

Figure 1

3. Fold and pin quilt right sides together at a 45-degree angle on one corner (Figure 2). Place a straightedge along the fold and lightly mark a line across the border ends.

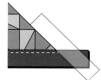

Figure 2

4. Stitch along the line, backstitching to secure. Trim seam to ¼" and press open (Figure 3).

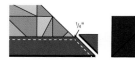

Figure 3

Quilt Backing & Batting

We suggest that you cut your backing and batting 8" larger than the finished quilt-top size. If preparing the backing from standard-width fabrics, remove the selvages and sew two or three lengths together; press seams open. If using 108"-wide fabric, trim to size on the straight grain of the fabric.

Prepare batting the same size as your backing. You can purchase prepackaged sizes or battings by the yard and trim to size.

Quilting

1. Press quilt top on both sides and trim all loose threads.

2. Make a quilt sandwich by layering the backing right side down, batting and quilt top centered right side up on flat surface and smooth out. Pin or baste layers together to hold.

3. Mark quilting design on quilt top and quilt as desired by hand or machine. ***Note:*** *If you are sending your quilt to a professional quilter, contact them for specifics about preparing your quilt for quilting.*

4. When quilting is complete, remove pins or basting. Trim batting and backing edges even with raw edges of quilt top.

Binding the Quilt

1. Join binding strips on short ends with diagonal seams to make one long strip; trim seams to ¼" and press seams open (Figure 4).

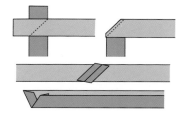

Figure 4

2. Fold 1" of one short end to wrong side and press. Fold the binding strip in half with wrong sides together along length, again referring to Figure 4; press.

3. Starting about 3" from the folded short end, sew binding to quilt top edges, matching raw edges and using a ¼" seam. Stop stitching ¼" from corner and backstitch (Figure 5).

Figure 5

4. Fold binding up at a 45-degree angle to seam and then down even with quilt edges, forming a pleat at corner, referring to Figure 6.

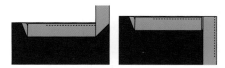

Figure 6

5. Resume stitching from corner edge as shown in Figure 6, down quilt side, backstitching ¼" from next corner. Repeat, mitering all

corners, stitching to within 3" of starting point.

6. Trim binding end long enough to tuck inside starting end and complete stitching (Figure 7).

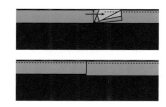

Figure 7

7. Fold binding to quilt back and stitch in place by hand or machine to complete your quilt.

Quilting Terms

- **Appliqué:** Adding fabric motifs to a foundation fabric by hand or machine (see Appliqué section of Basic Techniques).

- **Basting:** This temporarily secures layers of quilting materials together with safety pins, thread or a spray adhesive in preparation for quilting the layers.

  Use a long, straight stitch to hand- or machine-stitch one element to another holding the elements in place during construction and usually removed after construction.

- **Batting:** An insulating material made in a variety of fiber contents that is used between the quilt top and back to provide extra warmth and loft.

- **Binding:** A finishing strip of fabric sewn to the outer raw edges of a quilt to cover them.

  Straight-grain binding strips, cut on the crosswise straight grain of the fabric (see Straight & Bias Grain Lines Illustration on page 46), are commonly used.

  Bias binding strips are cut at a 45-degree angle to the straight grain of the fabric. They are used when binding is being added to curved edges.

- **Block:** The basic quilting unit that is repeated to complete the quilt's design composition. Blocks can be pieced, appliquéd or solid and are usually square or rectangular in shape.

- **Border:** The frame of a quilt's central design used to visually complete the design and give the eye a place to rest.

- **Fabric Grain:** The fibers that run either parallel (lengthwise grain) or perpendicular (crosswise grain) to the fabric selvage are straight grain.

   Bias is any diagonal line between the lengthwise or crosswise grain. At these angles the fabric is less stable and stretches easily. The true bias of a woven fabric is a 45-degree angle between the lengthwise and crosswise grain lines.

- **Mitered Corners:** Matching borders or turning bindings at a 45-degree angle at corners.

- **Patchwork:** A general term for the completed blocks or quilts that are made from smaller shapes sewn together.

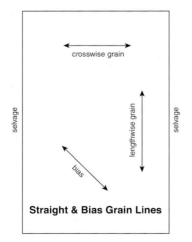

Straight & Bias Grain Lines

- **Pattern:** This may refer to the design of a fabric or to the written instructions for a particular quilt design.

- **Piecing:** The act of sewing smaller pieces and/or units of a block or quilt together.

   Paper or foundation piecing is sewing fabric to a paper or cloth foundation in a certain order.

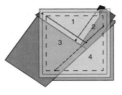

Foundation Piecing

   String or chain piecing is sewing pieces together in a continuous string without clipping threads between sections.

String or Chain Piecing

- **Pressing:** Pressing is the process of placing the iron on the fabric, lifting it off the fabric and placing it down in another location to flatten seams or crease fabric without sliding the iron across the fabric.

   Quilter's do not usually use steam when pressing, since it can easily distort fabric shapes.

   Generally, seam allowances are pressed toward the darker fabric in quilting so that they do not show through the lighter fabric.

   Seams are pressed in opposite directions where seams are being joined to allow seams to butt against each other and to distribute bulk.

   Seams are pressed open when multiple seams come together in one place.

   If you have a question about pressing direction, consult a

comprehensive quilting guide for guidance.

- **Quilt (noun):** A sandwich of two layers of fabric with a third insulating material between them that is then stitched together with the edges covered or bound.

- **Quilt (verb):** Stitching several layers of fabric materials together with a decorative design. Stippling, crosshatch, channel, in-the-ditch, free-motion, allover and meandering are all terms for quilting designs.

Meandering   **Stitch-in-the-ditch**

Channel   **Outline**

- **Quilt sandwich:** A layer of insulating material between a quilt's top and back fabric.

- **Rotary cutting:** Using a rotary cutting blade and straightedge to cut fabric.

- **Sashing:** Strips of fabric sewn between blocks to separate or set off the designs.

- **Subcut:** A second cutting of rotary-cut strips that makes the basic shapes used in block and quilt construction.

- **Template:** A pattern made from a sturdy material which is then used to cut shapes for patchwork and appliqué quilting. ∎